DISCARDED

JUN   4 2025

Asheville-Buncombe
Technical Community College
Learning Resources Center
340 Victoria Road
Asheville, NC 28801

Journey to Wholeness

D1523480

Asheville-Buncombe
Technical Community College
Learning Resources Center
340 Victoria Road
Asheville, NC 28801

Journey to Wholeness

Healing from the Trauma of Rape

Monique Lang

Learning Publications, Inc.
Holmes Beach, Florida

ISBN 1-55691-147-5

© 2000 by Monique Lang

All rights reserved. No part of this book may be reproduced or transmitted in any form or by any means, electronic or mechanical, including photocopying and recording, or by any information or retrieval systems, without permission in writing from the publisher.

Learning Publications, Inc.
5351 Gulf Drive
P.O. Box 1338
Holmes Beach, FL 34218-1338

Printing: 5 4 3 2 1   Year: 4 3 2 1 0

Printed in the United States of America

Dedication

To all the women who had the courage and the willingness to trust me with their story and to all who encouraged and supported me in bringing this book to actualization. Thank you. May you walk in beauty always.

Contents

Part 1

Part 2

Preface

The words "victim" and "survivor" are both used in this book because at the time of the rape you are a victim. However, now you are a survivor, and as you work through this book you will come to appreciate yourself more and more for having made it through the emotional, mental, and physical trauma of rape.

Journey to Wholeness is a self-help workbook. It is not the same as talking with a counselor, nor is it meant to take the place of a counselor.

If you are having emotional or physical problems due to the trauma of your rape, or are dealing with any issue triggered by having been raped, do seek professional help. It is a tremendous act of courage, but well worth the effort. Rape-crisis centers are listed in most phone directories and are equipped to provide you with the services that you might need.

How to Use This Book

This workbook is designed to be both educational and therapeutic.

Each chapter focuses on a particular rape-related topic, gives facts and information about rape and it's effect on the survivors, and guides you through a series of self-reflective exercises that involve thinking, feeling, and writing.

These exercises are meant to help you review the circumstances and situations of your rape and its aftermath, to shed a different perspective on your experience, to validate your actions, thoughts and feelings, and to help heal the wounds and scars of your rape.

This book is in two sections.

Part 1 is for those of you who were raped a while back and who are dealing mostly with the mental and emotional repercussions of having been violated.

Part 2 is specifically designed for those who were recently raped. This part provides information about matters that require prompt attention such as obtaining practical and emotional support from family and friends, securing medical care, and whether or not to report the rape to the police and prosecute the offender.

Introduction

Rape is a traumatic occurrence. You cannot prepare for it, and it marks your life in incomprehensible ways. The physical, mental, and emotional ramifications may take quite a while to get sorted, evaluated, and healed.

In writing this book I hope to offer to you some of the comfort and hope that many women have found in our counseling sessions. I am indebted to them for their openness, their trust, their willingness, their courage, and for teaching me.

Learning to heal the wounds of rape has evolved from years of working with rape survivors. It is my attempt to reach those of you who for whatever reason may not have had the opportunity to have personal counseling or for whom a book and some solitude are the best remedy. I hope this workbook will be both informative and healing.

It was natural that this book would evolve into workbook form because active participation such as talking, writing, drawing, and moving around, is often an important aspect of releasing feelings and healing.

Your reaction to the rape is an individual expression. You may have wanted to simply put the experience behind you. You may have tried to pretend that your rape never happened at all. You may have tried to deal with your thoughts and feelings but didn't quite know how to go about it. You probably have found that memories keep disrupting your life.

Each rape is different. Nonetheless there are certain responses and repercussions that are experienced by many survivors.

Journey to Wholeness is meant to inform you of the different issues and reactions that follow a rape. This will help you to normalize your experience and to feel that you are not the only one going through these experiences.

There also are exercises to guide you through your memories, thoughts, and feelings. These exercises are meant to help you put the emotional and mental remnants of the experience behind you.

If you chose to just read through the book without doing the exercises, that's fine. However, you will derive great benefit in doing. Give it a try, you might be surprised.

What this book asks of you may be difficult to tackle. It will take courage. So, go at your own pace and in your own way. Be gentle and compassionate with yourself.

This book is for you. What you write or draw in it is private. No one else needs to see it, unless you chose to share it with someone you trust and who can be there to support you.

And finally, consult a rape counselor if you are having difficulties. There are rape-crisis centers all over the nation. Their services are confidential and many are free.

Part 1

1
Self-Care Techniques

Many of us know how to take care of ourselves in nurturing ways; many of us do not. The following is a list of self-care techniques that can be helpful.

The techniques are not presented in any particular order. Experiment with those that seem most appealing to you. If you like them, check them off so that you can easily find them. At the end, add other techniques you have found helpful in the past.

When you feel the need for TLC (tender loving care) check your list. We generally forget what will make us feel good when we most need it.

- find a quiet place where you will be undisturbed
- turn off the phone
- listen to music
- go for a walk
- take a bath or shower
- talk to someone you trust
- read a book
- drink a cup of tea, coffee, or a soft drink
- go for a ride
- take a nap
- play sports
- meditate
- go shopping
- cry
- dance
- watch television
- seek support

- clean your home
- cook
- do a project that you enjoy
- exercise
- write
- draw, paint
- play an instrument
- sing
- add other items that make you feel good
- _____
- _____
- _____

Remember, it is always appropriate to ask for comfort. Giving and receiving comfort is one of the pleasures of being human.

Meditation Techniques

There are many meditation techniques. The goal of most of them is to quiet the body and the mind. There are many meditation books, tapes, and classes available.

Following are two of the most popular. Both involve sitting or lying down in a quiet place, undisturbed for at least 10 minutes. If you feel nervous about the time, set a timer. You can always continue if you feel unfinished.

Technique 1

Lie on your back or sit in an upright position with your back straight but not tight. Place both feet flat on the ground and your hands open and resting comfortably on your knees.

Close your eyes. If this is uncomfortable for you, look in an unfocused way at a point towards the floor.

Become aware of your breathing without changing it and slowly allow it to become deeper and slower. Keep aware of your breath coming into and leaving your body. You might want to think "in" on the inhale and "out" on the exhale. Allow your breathing to slow. If you experience feelings you do not want, you can let them come out on the exhale. You might want to add words like:

- Breathing in, I breath in peace (love, compassion, light, etc.)

- Breathing out, I exhale hurt (hate, anger, fear, etc.)

Keep repeating the phrases until you feel better.

Don't worry about intruding distractions. Just let them pass through your mind the way you see clouds pass through the sky and return your attention to your breathing. Gently.

Technique 2

Another common technique is to relax the body.

You begin the same way as in Technique 1 by sitting or lying down in a quiet place. Focus on your breathing. Then, beginning with your feet, slowly go through your body, directing each part to relax. For example:

Relax your toes . . . Relax your feet . . . Relax your ankles . . . and so on until you reach the top of your head.

Do the exercise slowly and deliberately.

2
Myths and Misconceptions

Eye Openers about Rape

Rape, rape victims, and rapists are misunderstood by society. The two most damaging ideas about rape are that rape is a sexual crime and that the victim is at fault.

In fact rape is a crime of violence in which sex is used as a weapon. It can happen to anyone, anywhere, and at anytime. Yet, we have been socialized to believe that rape happens only to certain kinds of people, and in certain circumstances. These deep-seated beliefs about rape may influence how you feel about yourself after being raped.

Reality often contrasts sharply to these stereotypic beliefs. Regardless of what you have been told or what you may think and feel now, you are not responsible for your rape. Rape is a forced sexual act. ***No one has the right to rape you or anyone else.*** No one wants to be raped.

Rape has nothing to do with seduction fantasies in which a woman, in her imagination, willingly gives her body for a pleasurable experience that she creates and controls.

Rape is a horrible violation. You were afraid. You had no control over the situation. To blame yourself for your rape is as ridiculous as putting the blame for a mugging attack on the person who was mugged. The following article from the American Bar Association demonstrates this illogical thinking.

Imagine how it might sound if a robbery victim were subjected to the kind of cross-examination as a rape victim:*

Attorney:	*Mr. Smith, you were held up at gunpoint on the corner of First and Main?*
Victim:	*Yes.*
A:	*Did you struggle with the robber?*
V:	*No.*
A:	*Why not?*
V:	*He was armed.*
A:	*Then you made a conscious decision to comply with his demands rather than resist?*
V:	*Yes.*
A:	*Did you scream? Cry out?*
V:	*No. I was afraid.*
A:	*I see. Have you ever been held up before?*
V:	*No.*
A:	*Have you ever **given** money away?*
V:	*Yes, of course.*
A:	*And you did so willingly?*
V:	*What are you getting at?*
A:	*Well, let's put it like this, Mr. Smith. You've given away moeny in the past. In fact, you have quite a reputation for philanthropy. How can we be sure you weren't **contriving** to have your money taken by force?*
V:	*Listen, if I wanted . . .*
A:	*Never mind. What time did the holdup take palce?*
V:	*About 11:00 p.m.*
A:	*You were out on the street at 11:00 p.m. Doing what?*
V:	*Just walking.*

---

*Reprinted with permission of the American Bar Association from the *ABA Journal* 61 (April 1975): 464.

A:	*Just walking? You know that it's dangerous being out on the street late at night. Weren't you aware that you could have been held up?*
V:	*I hadn't thought about it.*
A:	*What were you wearing at the time, Mr. Smith?*
V:	*Let's see . . . a suit. Yes, a suit.*
A:	*An **expensive** suit?*
V:	*Well . . . yes. I'm a successful lawyer, you know.*
A:	*In other words, Mr. Smith, you were walking around the streets late at night in a suit that practically advertised the fact that you might be a good target for some easy money, isn't that so? I mean, if we didn't know better, Mr. Smith, we might even think that you were **asking** for this to happen, mightn't we?*

If stereotypes about rape are misleading, why are they so pervasive? Because they give us a sense of security however false that sense might be. Each of us is a potential victim. To accept the myths is to believe the illusion that we, and those we love, won't be raped (victimized) if we avoid stereotypic behaviors and situations.

The following exercises are designed to help you recognize your beliefs and stereotypes about rape.

You are invited to express the ideas about rape that you had *before you were raped*. Make sentences, and/or picture arrangements around the words we have written in the middle of the pages that follow.

Also as you read through magazines you might want to clip out passages and/or photos that invoke some thought or feeling about your rape. Keep them in an envelope for use elsewhere in this workbook.

Write, draw, and/or cut and paste illustrations that show your *preconceptions* of **who** is a rape victim.

The Victim

Write, draw, and/or cut and paste illustrations that show your *preconceptions* or *beliefs* about **who** are rapists and what they are like.

The Rapist

Write, draw, and/or cut and paste illustrations to show your *preconceptions* or ideas of the *places* and *conditions* in which rapes occur.

Where

Write, draw, and/or cut and paste illustrations to show your *preconceptions* of **when** rapes occur. for example, time of day and situations.

When

Write, draw, and/or cut and paste illustrations to show your *preconceptions* of **why** people get raped.

Why

These exercises allowed you to become aware of your own stereotypical attitudes about rape. They are not bad attitudes. They are simply a product of your background, how you were taught, the books that you have read, and the television shows that you have watched. In short, these attitudes result from the impact of your world upon you.

The next chapter gives you the facts about rape. You also will have a chance to examine the difference between your preconceived ideas and what actually happened to you.

3
Facts About Rape

In the last chapter, we looked at the myths and the misconceptions of rape. Now we shall talk about the facts: the when, where, and why rapes occur, who are the victims and who are the rapists.

These facts will help you to realize that your own experience may parallel the experiences of many others. Knowing these facts might also help you feel better about yourself and dispel some self doubts.

For example, one woman was careful never to go into town alone at night because she believed that it was dangerous and that she could get into trouble. She believed that if she followed those rules she would be safe. She was raped in the middle of the day, while jogging in her neighborhood, by a married neighbor. All of her preconceptions about rape turned out not to apply to her situation. Knowing the facts helped her make sense of what felt like a completely distorted situation.

The second part of this chapter provides you with the opportunity to put your own experience into context and helps you to differentiate between the myths you might have previously believed and the facts of your experience.

Facts

Rape is any forcible sexual contact. This is true whether the threat was physical, mental, or emotional, obvious or subtle.

Who Are the Victims?

Victims are:

- as young as a few months old and as old as 97 years

- found in **all** social, racial, and ethnic groups
- usually of the same racial background as their rapist
- often acquainted with or recognized their rapist (more than 50 percent of the time)
- of any physical appearance
  » short and tall
  » fat and thin
  » blonde, brunette, redhead, etc.
- dressed in all attire, from dress up clothes to grungy sweatsuits
- single or married
- male or female

In other words, **anyone can be a victim at any time.**

Who Are the Rapists?

Rapists are:

- no different in appearance from anyone else
- seldom crazy or deranged looking
- often are acquainted with or recognize their victim.

They may even be your:

- neighbor
- date
- delivery man
- relative
- doctor
- teacher
- babysitter
- therapist
- boyfriend
- coworker
- spouse
- service man
- girlfriend's boyfriend
- family friend
- person on the bank line

- often of the same racial background as the victim
- married or single
- not sexually starved or frustrated, more than 50 percent are having sex regularly
- men or women

When Do Rapes Occur?

Whenever the rapist chooses.

Where Do Rapes Occur?

Wherever the rapist chooses.

Why Rapes Occur?

Rape is **not motivated by sex** or a sudden uncontrollable sexual urge. Most rapes are planned even when the victim has not been chosen ahead of time.

Rape is motivated by

- a combination of hostility and need to dominate
- a need to control and exercise power
- a sense of insecurity or inferiority
- a need to prove one's self
- revenge
- a desire to humiliate
- a rationalization that the victim is "asking for it"

The purpose of this chapter is to challenge stereotypes about rape. It will help you to put your thoughts onto paper.

What information on the preceding pages surprises you?

_____

_____

_____

_____

_____

What information have you found particularly significant or helpful?

_____

_____

_____

_____

_____

_____

Facts About Rape: Your Experience

Now that you have looked at your preconceptions about rape and have had a chance to consider the facts, you are invited to deliberately recall what happened to you when you were raped, in as many details as possible. The process of looking openly and honestly at what happened to you in detail may be stressful. However, the experiences of women in counseling emphasize that the process of telling your story will ease the burden of keeping it a secret.

Even if you have already told your story, I encourage you to do the exercises. Putting your story onto paper is another way of getting the thoughts, feelings, and memories out of your system and accelerate the healing process.

Before you begin, find a place in which you feel safe ---- a place where you know that you will not be disturbed (your favorite chair, a private room, under a tree, by the water, in your car, or any place that is safe and comforting for you). Give yourself enough time, at least an hour, to reflect upon your rape and to allow your emotions to surface.

Also, allow some time to relax before having to deal with any outside demands. At the end of the chapter there are more suggestions as to what you might do to help you feel better.

Write, draw, and/or cut and paste illustrations to represent *who you are.*

Write, draw, and/or cut and paste to illustrate who and what *your rapist* was like.

Write, draw, and/or cut and paste to illustrate **where** your rape occurred.

Write, draw, and/or cut and paste to illustrate **when** your rape occurred.

Write , draw, and/or cut and paste to illustrate **why** you think the person raped you.

Write, draw, and/or cut and paste to show **what** happened to you.

Recalling the particular circumstances of your rape may have felt liberating and cleansing. You might be feeling relieved and lighter. Those feelings are normal and appropriate.

On the other hand, the recollections may have stirred up a multitude of unpleasant and/or difficult thoughts and feelings. These feelings, too, are normal and appropriate, even if you wished you didn't have them or that they were different.

In either case, take a short break before you go on with your day or to the next chapter. You might want to walk around and stretch a bit, have a snack, sit quietly, scream and holler, jump around, breath deeply, call a friend —— or any activity that will help you feel good.

4
The Aftermath

One of the troubling aspects of rape is that we have been taught and conditioned to believe that it is a terrible thing. It **is** a terrible, life-changing event.

Nonetheless, there are times in which rape is not the violent, vicious attack that we are conditioned to believe it is. Even then it still does not make it right for someone to force you to have sex. As a result, you may have had or still have some conflicting feelings about the experience ---- particularly if the person who raped you was someone you knew.

For example, the person who raped you might have been gentle and caring. He may have told you that he cared about you, that you were beautiful, that you made him feel good, that you were wonderful, that he would like to see you again. He may even have been comforting and supportive.

You might have experienced conflicted feelings during the actual experience. You might have felt scared, disgusted, woozy, violated, repulsed, and/or you might have felt wanted, excited, cared for, loved. You might even have had an orgasm, whether you wanted to or not. (Orgasm can be an involuntary bodily response to stimulation and does not necessarily indicate enjoyment.) All of these feelings simply occur. They are not bad or good. They are just your feelings, and it is important to honor them ---- not to judge them.

Take some time now to reflect on whatever feelings you have or had. You might want to write or draw about them or talk to someone you trust.

Write, draw, and/or cut and paste to illustrate your thoughts and feelings from during and immediately after you were raped.

Write, draw, and/or cut and paste to illustrate your thoughts and feelings about your rape now.

Use this space to write or draw to show any conflicting thoughts or feelings.

One of the aftermaths of being raped is that we respond to certain situations and everyday events and stimuli in ways that seem odd, confusing, and unexplainable. For example, one woman could not understand why she felt nauseous every time she sat on her aunt's couch until she realized that the fabric was very similar to the surface on which she had been raped. After that insight, she stopped sitting on the couch altogether and no longer felt silly or embarrassed about it.

The following exercises are meant to help you make your own connections between thoughts, feelings, reactions, and ideas that may not make sense to you on the surface, and the possibility that they are being triggered by stimuli connected to what happened immediately before, during or soon after you were raped. For example, a smell, touch, sound, sight, or some other stimulus. Recognizing these connections will help you to understand your reactions, to be less troubled by their occurrence, and to know how to manage them in a way that works for you.

What specific **colors** can you remember from the times immediately before, during, and after your rape?

_____

_____

_____

_____

_____

_____

What specific **sounds** can you remember from the times during, immediately before and after your rape?

_____

_____

_____

_____

_____

_____

What specific **smells** can you remember from the times during, immediately before and after your rape?

_____

_____

_____

_____

_____

_____

What specific **tastes** can you remember from the times during, immediately before and after your rape?

_____

_____

_____

_____

_____

_____

What specific **words** can you remember from the times during, immediately before and after your rape?

_____

_____

_____

_____

_____

_____

What specific **gestures** can you remember from the times during, immediately before and after your rape?

_____

_____

_____

_____

_____

_____

What specific **textures** can you remember from the times during, immediately before and after your rape?

_____

_____

_____

_____

_____

_____

What specific **objects** can you remember from the times during, immediately before and after your rape?

_____

_____

_____

_____

_____

_____

Now that you have focused on the circumstantial and sensory details of your rape, do any of your previously "unexplainable" reactions to everyday stimuli make more sense? _____

Which ones?

_____

_____

_____

_____

_____

_____

Making these connections between your rape and your responses to present day stimuli should reassure you that your reactions are indeed normal and understandable. These exercises may have been hard to complete. You might be feeling emotionally, mentally, and/or physically drained. Respect these experiences. So many of us expect to go through intense situations quickly and return to our usual routine without missing a beat. Although this is the model that many in our society hold as admirable, it is not realistic and can usually only be achieved at great emotional and/or physical costs.

Give yourself some time to recuperate. Think of the things that have helped you feel better in the past (taking a bath, going for a walk, listening to music, talking to a friend, having a cup of coffee, reading a book, watching television, exercising, etc.) and do at least one of them. If you can't remember any, refer to Chapter 1. Take your time and be loving and gentle with yourself. As you go about your everyday life and progress through this workbook, more and more details having to do with your rape will pop up. Come back to this workbook and add more details, connections, and categories of your own.

5
You Are a Survivor

Many women look back at the events of their rape and feel that they did all that they could have or should have done. Many others feel that they could have or should have behaved differently than they did. This chapter emphasizes that there is no right or wrong way to behave at the time of a rape. However you conducted yourself, it was the right course of action.

At the time of your rape you were a victim. Someone was imposing his will and forcing himself on you. Now you are a **survivor.** You have regained or are regaining control over your life.

When you were raped, you were, most likely, confused or frightened. Whether you were raped by a stranger, by someone which you recognized, by a friend, or by someone you were dating, there were clues of danger. Some of these may have been almost imperceptible: a tone of voice, a look in the eye, or a certain indescribable demeanor that can be as threatening and disarming as a physical weapon or brute force ---- even the threat that you would be called a slut in the morning if you didn't agree to have sex. In acquaintance or date rape, the threat can be as subtle as the fear of embarrassment or not knowing how to say "no" forcefully enough.

In the case of rape by a stranger, you often do not even have the time to think clearly before he begins to rape you. You may not know whether he has a weapon or how strong he is. In fact, most men are stronger than most women and can easily overpower them. Plus, there is the element of surprise. Yelling, screaming, fighting, fleeing may not be possible. And, most importantly, you do not know at that terrifying moment whether attempting to defend yourself would actually help you escape, or whether it would create a situation in which more force and greater physical harm might result.

In acquaintance and date rape, feelings can be jumbled. Many women disbelieve that the rape is even taking place. They may have said "no" only to have their refusal disregarded. Or the rapist might have insisted that the woman really "wanted it" and that she should just admit that she wanted it. Sometimes the rapist threatens to disclose information to others that would be embarrassing, at best, and possibly damaging, even if the information is untrue. The rapist knows that it is easier for him to tell a lie about you than it is for you to defend yourself against that lie.

In cases of extreme stress, our conscious, rational mind often becomes muddled, and our unconscious, intuitive mind takes over. Our survival instinct resides in the unconscious; therefore, we act and react intuitively to protect ourselves as effectively as possible. It is vital that you understand and believe that, however you reacted to the situation, you did the right thing. Unconsciously, your instincts took over and determined your actions. If you struggled, it was "right." If you didn't struggle, that, too, was the "right" reaction. If you did a combination of things, they also were appropriate. Counselors have a maxim that they like to pass on to their clients: "Don't should on yourself." Dealing with rape and its aftermath is one situation in which the admonition to "not should upon oneself" applies. Don't second guess yourself, either. If you could have behaved differently, you would have.

One of my clients was upset that she had not kicked and screamed, when, in fact, her rapist had tied her ankles together and was holding a pillow over her face. Yet, she maintained that if she had yelled, she would not have been raped.

Listen carefully to your own voice. Others cannot tell you how you should have behaved under those circumstances, because they were not with you when the rape occurred. They cannot fully understand what the situation was like. Additionally, each of us is unique, and we handle danger differently, just as we handle life differently. The ways of others are not necessarily better or worse, they just are not your way.

The exercises on the following pages will help you to consider your actions at the time of your rape, and to clarify the possible options and the consequences of acting differently. As with all the exercises in this book, take your time and be compassionate with yourself.

These exercises may bring up punitive thoughts and feelings. Please talk to someone you trust if this happens to you, or if the exercises bring up intense feelings that upset you for more than a day or so.

Write, draw, or cut and paste to show what you did when your rapist approached you.

Do you believe you should have acted differently?

_____

How?

_____

_____

_____

_____

_____

_____

_____

Why?

_____

_____

_____

_____

_____

_____

_____

Do you think you **could** have acted differently?

_____

How?

_____

_____

_____

_____

_____

_____

_____

What do you think would have happened if you had acted that way?

_____

_____

_____

_____

_____

_____

_____

If you had acted as you think you should have/could have, would your safety, survival, or well-being have been guaranteed?

_____

_____

_____

_____

_____

If you had acted as you think you should have/could have, might you have suffered even more?

_____

How?

_____

_____

_____

_____

_____

_____

Hopefully, answering the above questions has convinced you that you acted in the most appropriate manner possible, considering the circumstances. It is also worthwhile to remember that most of us have 20/20 hindsight. It is one thing to consider a situation from a position of calm and detachment and quite another to have to respond in a situation in which your life may be in danger. Remember, in times of danger our unconscious takes over and determines our best course of action for survival.

It is time to reaffirm to yourself that **you are a survivor.**

Write **"I am a survivor!"** three times.

_____

_____

_____

Now, say the words out loud. "I am a survivor!" Say the words three times.

Make the statement that "I am a survivor!" out loud and mean it.

Repeat the statement, emphasizing the bold-face word.

- **I** am a survivor!
- I **am** a survivor!
- I am a **survivor!**

Write how it feels to think of yourself as a survivor.

_____

_____

_____

_____

Write how this differs from thinking of yourself as a victim?

_____

_____

_____

_____

Did this exercise feel empowering and wonderful? Did it feel like a silly and useless exercise? Did it feel like a lie or a pretension? Regardless of how the exercise felt to you, honor your feelings. Your feelings are neither right nor wrong. Nor are they an expression of how well you're doing in your recovery. They simply are your feelings.

You may feel quite comfortable experiencing yourself as a survivor. You might even have done so from the beginning ---- or you might still feel that it's a challenge to make the switch in your mind. Doubt may keep rearing its ugly head. That, too, is normal. Changes in points of view seldom happen overnight. Just keep looking at the events as a survivor, rather than as a victim. This viewpoint will take you a long way into healing.

With that in mind, try to recall a time when you felt good about yourself.

Write, draw, and/or cut and paste to illustrate your thoughts about that time.

Remember. You are still that person.

6
Post Traumatic Stress Syndrome

Rape victims frequently fear that they are going crazy because they are feeling and acting in ways that are unfamiliar to themselves and others. Coping with daily life becomes more difficult. This cluster of thoughts, feelings, and behaviors is the normal response to the trauma of rape. It is called Rape Trauma Syndrome or Post Traumatic Stress Disorder (PTSD).

Rape survivors pass through recognizable physical, behavioral, and emotional stages on their way to recovery. Some stages overlap. One behavior will remain, while another one changes or disappears, while yet another appears. This can be quite frustrating, because the overlapping might make you feel that there is no end to the confusion, but there will be. You will pass through these stages in your own way and on your own time schedule. You will achieve your own unique resolution and regain a personally suitable lifestyle.

Rape Trauma Syndrome comprises three major and commonly identified stages.

Acute Phase

This cluster of physical and emotional reactions occurs immediately following the attack and may last for a few days or several weeks. These reactions also can arise when a rape long undealt with, or forgotten, is remembered.

Transition Phase

This phase overlaps and follows the Acute Reaction. During the transition, you might be trying to make sense of the incomprehensible. It is a time of questioning and regrouping.

Reorganization and Integration Phase

During this phase, life settles into a new normalcy. Upsets in behaviors, feelings, and thoughts are more the exception than the norm. It might be helpful for you to think of these phases the way one of my clients did. After going through all three stages, she said it reminded her of when she had an emergency appendectomy as a child. At first (Acute Phase) most of her attention focused on the surgery, her incision, what she could and couldn't do, how it hurt, and how other people reacted to her. Then (Transition Phase) she remembered being aware of the wound when she bent over, lifted heavy things, or sneezed hard. She wanted to know why her appendix had gone bad, how long it would take for her to be all better. She felt angry and frustrated that it took so long to heal. Then (Reorganization and Integration Phase) her life was back to normal. Now, she occasionally notices the scar when she takes a shower or tries on a two-piece bathing suit.

Although each person is unique, there are some common consequences that result from being raped. Below is a list of some physical symptoms, thoughts, feelings, and behaviors experienced by rape survivors. They are neither "good" nor "bad." You may have had some of them, have them now, or may never have them. These physical symptoms, thoughts, feelings, and behaviors may occur both in the Acute and Transition Phases with varying degrees of severity.

It is difficult to precisely differentiate the stages of Rape Trauma Syndrome, because many of the symptoms are the same during each phase. The difference is in the intensity with which they are experienced. As you move toward transition and then integration, the physical symptoms often lessen, and the thoughts and feelings take on a different tone. For example, many survivors will go from "shock" to "anger" or from thinking "why me?" to "how could he do this to me?" It is not really important to know what stage you're in. What matters is knowing that what you are feeling and experiencing is normal. Remember, you are a separate individual. Your experience was unique, and so are your responses.

As you read the following pages, you might want to check off the physical symptoms, thoughts, feelings, and behaviors that fit you now, or those that you may have experienced in the past. As time goes by, you can modify the list as you wish. The list might give you an overview of what you've been through and the progress that you have made.

Physical Symptoms

- ■ Pain
  - ☐ all over
  - ☐ head
  - ☐ neck and shoulders
  - ☐ upper/lower back
  - ☐ mouth
  - ☐ breasts
  - ☐ arms
  - ☐ wrists/hands
  - ☐ abdomen
  - ☐ pelvis
  - ☐ vagina
  - ☐ anus
  - ☐ thighs/buttocks
  - ☐ legs
  - ☐ ankles
  - ☐ inner organs
- ☐ klutziness
- ☐ muscle tension
- ☐ shaking
- ☐ fill in any not mentioned above
- ☐ _____
- ☐ _____

- ☐ numbness
- ☐ stiffness
- ☐ nausea
- ☐ stomach ache
- ☐ headaches
- ☐ dizziness
- ☐ loss of appetite
- ☐ increased appetite
- ☐ fatigue
- ☐ sweating
- ☐ palpitations
- ☐ sensitivity to light
- ☐ sensitivity to sound
- ☐ sensitivity to touch
- ☐ sensitivity to taste
- ☐ sensitivity to smell
- ☐ stuttering
- ☐ insomnia
- ☐ inertia
- ☐ night sweats
- ☐ _____
- ☐ _____
- ☐ _____

There also may be side effects to the medications that you are taking to help you through this traumatic time. Most pharmacies provide printed information about the side effects of the prescriptions they dispense. If you are unsure whether what you are experiencing results from the medication, check with your physician. Your can also call your local rape-crisis center for general information. What is important is, you do not need to be in greater discomfort than you have to be. Many medications can be exchanged for others and be just as effective, without the deleterious side effects.

Thoughts

- ☐ What's happening to me?
- ☐ I must be going crazy!
- ☐ I don't want to deal with this anymore.
- ☐ I want it to go away.
- ☐ I can't believe this happened to me.
- ☐ It didn't really happen.
- ☐ This is the worst thing that's ever happened to me.
- ☐ Why me?
- ☐ It must be my fault.
- ☐ If only I had . . .
- ☐ If only I hadn't . . .
- ☐ Overacting.
- ☐ He'll come back to get me.
- ☐ What will people think of me?
- ☐ I didn't know people could be so awful.
- ☐ No one understands.
- ☐ If I start to cry, I'll never stop.
- ☐ At least I'm alive.
- ☐ I'm so ashamed I can't get rid of him.
- ☐ I can't stand the pain.
- ☐ I'll show them!
- ☐ I'm okay, I'm strong.
- ☐ Will I ever be myself again?
- ☐ Will this always haunt me?
- ☐ Was he HIV+?

Use the rest of this page to add any thoughts of your own.

_____

_____

_____

_____

Feelings

- ■ Fears of
  - ☐ the rapist
  - ☐ V.D.
  - ☐ pregnancy
  - ☐ being alone
  - ☐ going crazy
  - ☐ the dark
  - ☐ the light
  - ☐ noise
  - ☐ silence
  - ☐ crowds
  - ☐ going to sleep
  - ☐ insomnia
  - ☐ taking a shower or bath
  - ☐ leaving home
  - ☐ staying home
  - ☐ television
  - ☐ movies
  - ☐ looking attractive
  - ☐ specific places
  - ☐ loosing control
  - ☐ reactions of family, coworkers, friends
  - ☐ men
  - ☐ AIDS
- ☐ embarrassed
- ☐ sorry for the rapist
- ☐ separated from reality
- ☐ obsessed by sex
- ☐ glad to be alive
- ☐ scared
- ☐ alone
- ☐ angry
- ☐ hurt
- ☐ guilty
- ☐ vulnerable
- ☐ crazy
- ☐ ugly
- ☐ dirty
- ☐ hopeless
- ☐ helpless
- ☐ exposed
- ☐ stigmatized
- ☐ impatient
- ☐ overwhelmed
- ☐ lost
- ☐ anxious
- ☐ confused
- ☐ sad
- ☐ disbelief
- ☐ depressed
- ☐ shock
- ☐ humiliated
- ☐ revengeful
- ☐ responsible for others
- ☐ disinterested in sex

Use the rest of this page to reflect upon your unique feelings and fears.

_____

_____

_____

Behaviors

- [ ] crying
- [ ] inappropriate laughing
- [ ] sarcasm
- [ ] excessive activity
    - [ ] cleaning
    - [ ] cooking
    - [ ] shopping
    - [ ] work
- [ ] insomnia
- [ ] lethargy
- [ ] foul language
- [ ] tired
- [ ] change in appearance
- [ ] hairstyle
- [ ] clothing
- [ ] make up
- [ ] drinking/drugging
- [ ] withdrawing
- [ ] seeking company
- [ ] increased sexual interest
- [ ] taking high risks

- [ ] compulsive washing
- [ ] giggles
- [ ] calmness
- [ ] can't get going
- [ ] irritability
- [ ] preoccupation with body
- [ ] rocking
- [ ] over eating
- [ ] increased sleep
- [ ] fidgety
- [ ] crankiness
- [ ] uninterested
- [ ] disorganized
- [ ] messy
- [ ] neat
- [ ] indecisive
- [ ] legal drug use
- [ ] compulsiveness
- [ ] lack of sexual interest
- [ ] preoccupation with safety

Use the rest of this space to note some of your own behaviors.

_____

_____

_____

_____

_____

_____

Now let's see how all of this applies to you. You may have identified with some of the symptoms listed and not with others. You also may have discovered some of your own symptoms. That's how it should be. Furthermore, you might find yourself thinking, feeling, and behaving in ways that seem strange and out of character for you. These peculiarities to your personality are actually a sane response to an insane situation. Rape is a situation that can turn our world's view upside down. It shatters our experience of being at least somewhat safe in this world. It, thus, makes sense that we should feel, think, and behave in ways that are unfamiliar to who we know ourselves to be.

Now might be the right time time to put all of this together for yourself, to note how your thoughts, feelings, and behaviors have changed and how your world's view may be skewed differently. If you are in the Reorganization and Integration Phase, the exercises on the last few pages may have been relatively easy for you. On the other hand you might have felt discouraged because your life is still not what you would like it to be. Hang in there. We all tend to become impatient when healing does not proceed according to our plan and expectations. It would be nice if I could assure you that tomorrow, or next week, or next month, you will be all better, but that's not possible. You are unique. You will heal in your own way and at your own pace. However, if you continue to work through your feelings, thoughts, and behaviors, as you have been doing, you will heal and return to a satisfactory lifestyle.

Sometimes, it is helpful to think back to other difficult periods in your life. Difficult events in your life could have been anything from a close friend moving away, surgery, an accident, the loss of a pet, a divorce, the death of someone you cared about, or any event that tumbled your life. Visiting the past in this way can help you to put the experience of being raped into a larger context. It also will reinforce the knowledge that you will not always feel the way you do now.

Recall and write about one or two difficult events in your life.

_____

_____

_____

_____

_____

_____

_____

How did you feel when it first happened?

_____

_____

_____

_____

_____

_____

What helped you feel better?

_____

_____

_____

_____

_____

Where/how did you get comfort?

_____

_____

_____

_____

_____

It can be reassuring to realize that you have already dealt with a difficult situation, even if the situation was not of this magnitude. You can now rely on some of the skills and tools that were helpful then ---- as well as any new coping skills that you have learned since.

As with all the exercises in this book, you may have found that your healing has progressed. Rejoice and feel good about yourself. You might want to find a way to acknowledge and to celebrate.

On the other hand, focusing on the areas of your life that still may not be integrated and healed might have triggered intense feelings. Do be kind to yourself. Give yourself some time to ease your discomfort. Again, you might want to seek out someone you trust to discuss your responses and the feelings they triggered. Seeking support is not sign of weakness, it is the mark of wisdom.

7
Dreams, Daydreams, Nightmares, and Flashbacks

Although dreaming is a universal occurrence, we know little about it. There are many theories about dreams. Freud called dreams the "royal road to the unconscious." Some religions consider them a way of communicating with angels and spirits. Some cultures believe that dreams represent a different reality.

What we do know is that we all dream. Some of us remember our dreams vividly upon waking. Others of us have a sense of having dreamed, but can't recall the dream. Some of us feel we haven't dreamed at all.

There are also many different types of dreams. Some seem like everyday life occurrences in which we meet the people that we know and do the things we would usually do in our daily life. Other dreams are more phantasmagoric. Things are wild, unlike anything that we are used to and the people we meet look and act in ways that are not familiar. Some dreams are pleasant and soothing, some uneventful. Some are highly charged emotionally; others are not. Some are quite frightening and upsetting. Those, as you well know, are called nightmares.

Daydreams occur while you're awake. Your mind wanders away from the present moment and the immediate reality. Daydreams also can occur in what is called the hypnagogic state which is the time between sleep and wakefulness and can be either right before going to sleep or just prior to being fully awake.

And there is the added factor of periodicity. You may recall your dreams vividly for a few days or months, not at all for a while, and then begin to remember again. Many theories try to explain why this is so, but, basically, no one quite knows for sure.

A challenging concept is that we actually are the author of our own dreams and that we create them to either learn something or work out a situation. The theory expands into the belief that we can consciously change our dreams.

This is how it works: You let yourself know before going to sleep that you are the director of your dreams and that you have the ability to change what is happening while you are dreaming. Then, while in the dream, you can give yourself instructions such as "this is a dream, I have a choice of how I want it to happen, and I want to change it this way," or "I know I am in a dream, and I am just going to watch what is going on, although I know it isn't the reality that I live in," or "This is a dream, and I want it to stop, go away." As crazy as it may sound, this technique of becoming the observer of your dreams often helps to diminish the fierceness of the nightmares and the dreams become less frightening. One young woman conquered horrible nightmares by telling them to go away when they started. It's worth a try.

Flashbacks tend to occur while in a state of wakefulness, during a daydream. You also may have flashback dreams. A flashback is what happens when we remember an experience as if it were happening in the present. Flashbacks can be pleasurable as well as scary.

A good technique to use in dealing with flashbacks in the awake state is to consciously and intensely focus on something in the present and concrete, such as clasping and unclasping your hands, listening to the tick of a clock, or focusing on an object in your field of vision. This will help you to consciously know where you are and what is going on in the moment. If someone is there with you, start a conversation. This will bring you back to reality and distract you from the images in your mind. If the person is someone you trust, tell the person that you are having a flashback. Talking about the flashback brings it into the open and makes it easier for you to get through it. If the flashback occurs in a dream state, then use the techniques for dealing with dreams that were mentioned in previous paragraphs. You might also wake yourself to check your present reality.

Daydreams, flashbacks, and dreams are common in the aftermath of a trauma, and survivors report having them. Quite often, the dreams have a nightmarish quality in which the dreamer is in some kind of danger or frightening situation, though not necessarily a rape. The dreams can seem very ordinary or highly "sci-fi." One kind of dream is no better or worse than any other. You will dream in the style that is best suited to who you are. One young woman had recurrent nightmares of two red eyes coming in through her bedroom window and shooting her with "The Force." As she became stronger and healthy, she fashioned an imaginary shield that not only protected her, but reflected "The Force" back to the assailant and disintegrated him.

In the aftermath of rape, there seems to be a sequence of common types of dreams that appear to have a natural progression as time passes and healing occurs. Dreams that leave you feeling like the helpless victim often come first. A common theme in these nightmares is that the dreamer is being pursued or attacked by a person, animal, or thing, and the dreamer does not have the capability to defend and save herself. One woman kept dreaming that she was walking in a crowd. She felt she was in danger, even though she couldn't see it or feel the source of the danger. There was no way out. Another dreamer was trapped in a car, another pursued by a monster. Regardless of the specifics of the dream, the dreamer wakes up in a panic and may be unable to go back to sleep or to feel safe in her space and/or body.

Later, such dreams may have endings in which the victim becomes a survivor. While in the midst of danger, she confronts the situation, seizes control, and saves herself. This shift often is a message that the dreamer is feeling stronger and less vulnerable. For example, the woman who dreamed she was stuck in a crowd, found an alleyway into which she escaped and safely arrived at her destination.

Many survivors are perplexed and upset when, in their dreams, they become revengeful and/or take on the role of attacker. Again, this is a healthy indication because appropriate anger towards the aggressor is safely expressed without anyone actually being harmed. It does not mean that the dreamer will become a violent, vicious person in the wakeful state. We all have the capacity for violence. The difference is that most of us chose not to act upon that capacity.

The following pages are provided for you to record the dates, as well as the themes, thoughts, and feelings that are present in your daydreams, dreams, and flashbacks. Writing them down actually helps to get them out of your head. This way they won't go around and around in your head so much. Also as a step towards your healing they might provide you with a valuable record of your recovery process.

If you are not dreaming, or not remembering your dreams, don't worry about it. Not everyone remembers their dreams, and it's not a necessary step in healing.

As in all other chapters, if you are having a hard time with any of this material, do contact someone you trust to talk to them about it, or if you don't know any one you feel you can trust with this material, call your local rape-crisis center to talk to a trained counselor.

Record your dreams, daydreams, nightmares, and flashbacks below. Use other paper as necessary.

_____

_____

_____

_____

_____

_____

_____

_____

_____

_____

_____

_____

_____

_____

_____

_____

_____

_____

8
"Speaking to" the Rapist

An important aspect of healing is to express all your thoughts and feelings. Communicating directly with your perpetrator is often quite impossible or unwise, even though you may have a few things to tell him! Here is a technique that offers you just that opportunity: Write him a letter. Write the letter, even if you don't know the rapist. As silly as it sounds to write a letter that might never be sent, it is a technique that has been used by many people, in many circumstances, with beneficial results. Besides, what have you got to lose?

Give yourself all the time that you need. You may complete the letter in one sitting, or you may see it as a work in progress and add to it over time. As with most other exercises in this book, find a quiet time and space, and then just start writing. Don't worry about your grammar, or whether you're making sense, or about repeating yourself, or the condition of your handwriting. Just allow your thoughts and feelings to pour out onto the paper. Many conflicting feelings may surface. That's fine. Put them all down: from anger to sadness, to fear, to hate, to compassion, to revenge, to sorrow. Keep writing for as long as necessary. It could be five minutes or five hours.

Once you're done you may chose to send the letter, keep it, burn it, tear it, or whatever satisfies you. Furthermore, you can write as many letters as you want or need to write to say all that you feel, or until you have said all that you want to say.

There may be other people with whom you have unfinished business: such as policemen, hospital personnel, district attorneys, doctors, counselors, relatives, friends, coworkers, or others. Feel free to write to them as well. Use the same process as above. As with the letter to your rapist, you have the option of sending it, or not.

Writing is definitely recommended as a technique to use in healing. However, if writing is just not your thing and you feel uncomfortable with it, use drawings or cut and paste as you have in the rest of this book. When you're done with your letter writing, use the next page to write how you feel now.

As with the other exercises in this book, if you're having a hard time while or after doing this exercise, seek support from someone you trust.

9
Impact on Family and Friends

Although you're the one who was raped, the impact and the reverberations of the event extend to those close to you ---- the secondary victims. Often, the closer the relationship, the greater the impact, whether or not they show it. They, too, may be flooded by thoughts and feelings that they can't understand or explain. For some, your experience might even have triggered the memory of their own rape or sexual abuse. (Remember that conservative statistics estimate that 50 percent of all women will have been sexually abused in their lifetime.)

Use this chapter to reflect on how you think your being raped has affected the people in your life, how it has impacted them, why they may be responding to you as they have been, and the effects it may have on your relationship.

Following is a list of common responses from secondary victims. Check off the ones that apply, or applied, to the people in your life.

- ❏ guilt that they couldn't protect you from the attack
- ❏ vengeance towards the rapist
- ❏ strong feelings about the reasons they think you were raped (some of which may be negative ---- remember the chapter on myths and misconceptions)
- ❏ specific ideas about how you should proceed
- ❏ a timetable for your healing and recovery
- ❏ overprotectiveness
- ❏ blaming you for the attack
- ❏ wanting to make everything better
- ❏ wanting to pretend that it didn't happen
- ❏ shame

- ❑ not wanting to talk about it
- ❑ treating you like an invalid
- ❑ feeling of powerlessness
- ❑ erratic behavior

Add any other responses that suit your particular situation.

_____

_____

_____

_____

Write, draw, and/or cut and paste illustrations to describe your thoughts and feelings about the behavior of the people in your life.

If your rape happened a long time ago, and you have just recently told the people close to you, other feelings may arise. Common feelings are: hurt and anger that you didn't tell them before; disbelief; wanting to do something about it now; denial.

Some people can be very supportive and understanding in the moment, then become unavailable over time, even annoyed that you are not back to "normal" on their timetable.

In this time of stress, it is not your job to take care of others. This is a particularly important fact to embrace if you are a natural caretaker. This is a time for you to be cared for ---- not the other way around. However, understanding that each person has her or his limitations and can only be who they are, will temper your expectations and ease your relationships. Relatives, friends and coworkers will usually respond in ways that are true to their characters. You may have some surprises, but, in general, people who have been supportive and understanding in the past will be so now.

We all have expectations about how the people in our lives will behave when we need them. It's hard when someone doesn't come through for us, especially in time of crisis. If that happens, you need to know that it's about them, not you. On the other hand, if you have a tendency to be completely self-reliant, you might break that pattern and reach out for help. You might be surprised at the support you receive (see Chapter 16).

The exercises on the following pages are designed to help you:

1) recognize your expectations of how those close to you would respond

2) recognize how they actually did respond

3) examine what might be going on for them

Make a list of the people from whom you expect support. What kind of support do you expect? What support are you actually getting?

Name	Expectations	Actual Support

In times of crisis, we all react differently. Your rape may have triggered old thoughts, feelings, and patterns in those close to you. The ghosts and goblins from their past might prevent them from being supportive to you. The attack upon you might awaken memories of their own rape or incest.

In coping with that, they may project their own needs onto you, as they deal with any of their unresolved feelings. They may feel powerless and disempowered. The situation may just be too painful or scary for them to deal with your needs and the reality of this new attack. Remember that it is not personal.

For the men in your life, your rape may make them feel that they weren't doing their job of protecting you, even if that wasn't possible. Some still believe that it's the woman's fault, even if they know better. Irrationally, some may feel that they were betrayed. There are many reasons why someone may not be as understanding and supportive as you would like them to be. Figuring out why might help. You might appreciate that it's not a lack of caring, but the inability to assist. On the other hand, some people just don't have the capacity to be there for anyone but themselves.

Write down the reasons you think some people are not giving you the support you want.

Name   **Reasons**

_____

_____

_____

_____

_____

How do you feel about their lack of support now?

_____

_____

_____

_____

_____

How have the people in your life been affected by your rape?

| | | **How Is this Person** |
Name	**Relationship**	**Being Affected**

Write, draw, and/or cut and paste illustrations to show how the impact on their lives affects the way they treat you.

Some people will have a heightened regard for you or feel closer to you because you were violated.

Write, draw, or cut and paste to illustrate your experience with those people and how you feel about it.

Unfortunately, some people will perceive you negatively and/or relate to you differently because you were raped.

Write, draw, or cut and paste to illustrate your reaction to that experience.

You might want to try to understand why their opinion of you has changed negatively. It might be related to what you discovered about them on pages 65 and 69.

Being raped is a crisis. Crises create stress. Stress in your personal life, stress in other people's lives and stress in your relationships. Stress is common. Stress is normal. Stress is difficult to manage. There are, however, some techniques that you can use to help lessen the tension and bring some ease into your life. A good first step is to remember what tactics worked for you in the past in coping with difficult periods in your life.

Write, draw, and/or cut and paste to show what tactics worked in the past.

If you have already tried your known ways of coping with the stress, and none of them seem to be working this time around, don't despair. This is a new crisis and you may simply need to look at, and work on, the problem in a new way.

One possibility is to talk with someone you respect and to seek that person's suggestions about what you might be able to do to cope more easily. The bonus is that simply talking may bring some relief and dissipate some of the tension. Talking might also prompt some new ideas and techniques in your own thinking.

If your relationships are stressed, try talking to the persons involved. Let them know that you are feeling that there is stress between you. Does the other person feel it too? Be as honest as possible about how you feel. Do they experience it the same way or do they view it differently? Try to be clear about what you expect from each person. Opening a dialogue is often the best way to resolve stress and conflict.

For many of us, it is quite a challenge to ask for what we need from our family and friends. However, people can't give us the support we need if they don't know we need it or how we need it. For one person, support might mean being left alone, for another being asked if they want a cup of tea. The responses vary with the individuals. Help those close to you be of help to you. Unfortunately, they aren't mindreaders and won't know what to give you unless you tell them. It's been my experience that if I can ask for what I need, most likely I will get it, and the people in my life will be pleased to have been asked and to provide.

Fill out the list in Chapter 16. Figure out who is best suited to fill each need. No one can be all things to all people. Knowing whom to ask for what is needed will make your life and theirs easier. This gives everyone a chance to share in the process, without overly burdening one person. It also will provide you with different types of backing, an important aspect in the healing process.

As hard as it may be, honor and respect that those close to you are also struggling with the events. They, too, have pain.

As ridiculous as this suggestion may seem to you at this time: *Try to make time to have fun and enjoy the people that you are with*. Even in times of crisis, taking a break and making the time to have a good time ---- whatever that means to you, keeps relationships flowing and is a vital part of the healing.

10
Medical Attention

Whether you were raped weeks ago, months ago, or years ago, the repercussions of receiving, or not receiving, medical attention, may still linger. This chapter is aimed at helping you to integrate your experience, whether you obtained medical care at the time of your rape, or chose to decline it.

For some women, the medical care provided was a positive experience. They felt respected and taken care of. For others, it was the opposite. The medical attention was insensitive at best. If your experience was not positive, it still may be preventing you from receiving the kind of routine medical care that supports good health. When was your last check up?

Routine yearly medical and gynecological check ups are part of health maintenance and disease prevention. If you have not had a check up within the last year or so, this chapter may be of particular importance ---- and difficulty ---- for you.

If this is a tender, difficult issue for you, you might choose to talk to a professional or someone you trust about it to resolve the obstacles that prevent you from getting routine medical care.

If you do not seek medical care because of religious or philosophical reasons that you held prior to your rape, then by all means continue to follow your conscience.

I want to emphasize, however, that it can be detrimental to refuse medical attention due to unresolved issues connected to your experience after your rape.

Write, draw, and/or cut and paste to illustrate the reasons and the circumstances that helped you to choose or not to choose medical attention after being raped.

Thinking back, how do you feel about your decision?

_____

_____

_____

_____

_____

_____

_____

_____

_____

_____

_____

_____

_____

_____

_____

_____

_____

_____

Regardless of the reasons why you chose to seek medical help, or not, it is important that you not make yourself wrong for that decision now. It was the best choice at the time. You need to honor your decision.

How you feel about the medical attention you received becomes a part of your healing process. Completing the statements below will help you express and integrate your thoughts and feelings about it.

This first set of open-ended statements is aimed at helping you to remember how you were treated. You are encouraged to complete the sentences.

The physicians were _____

_____

_____

_____

_____

The nurses were _____

_____

_____

_____

_____

The surroundings were _____

_____

_____

_____

_____

Treatment was _____

_____

_____

_____

_____

I'm glad that   _____

_____

_____

_____

_____

I'm sad/angry/   _____

upset that   _____

_____

_____

_____

This set of open-ended sentences is to help you identify how you wish you had been treated if your experience was not a positive one. Complete the sentences.

I wish the doctors had been   _____

_____

_____

_____

_____

I wish the nurses had been   _____

_____

_____

_____

_____

I wish treatment had been _____

_____

_____

_____

_____

I wish that _____

_____

_____

_____

_____

Write, draw, and/or cut and paste to illustrate your overall thoughts and feelings about the medical treatment you received.

Write, draw, and/or cut and paste to show the reasons you are not receiving routine medical attention now.

Write, draw, and/or cut and paste to illustrate what would help you to overcome the obstacles to getting a routine physical examination.

Pick the *easiest* action for you to take toward getting some routine care, be it a simple check up, a Pap test, or a mammogram, and plan to do it within the next month (today or tomorrow is good, too). Remember that when you call for an appointment, chances are, it will be several weeks before a physician will be able to see you, unless you have specific symptoms. This will give you time to prepare for the visit.

You have just completed an important step towards your own recovery. You may be experiencing a jumble of thoughts and feelings. Whatever those thoughts and feelings are, they are appropriate to the situation, though they may seem strange to you. These thoughts, feelings, and behaviors are a predictable part of what is known as Rape Trauma Syndrome (see Chapter 6).

So, before you do anything else, take some time to relax and to acknowledge yourself for doing these exercises.

11
Reporting the Crime

Whether you reported your rape to the police or whether you didn't, in retrospect you may feel pleased with your choice or you may wish that you had elected a different option. Regardless of what your choice was, it is important that you understand and acknowledge that you made the best decision for yourself at that time. The goal of this chapter is to help you appreciate the choice that you made and to integrate the experience that followed.

The first set of exercises is designed to help you to recognize and to understand the reasons you made the choice you did. If you reported the rape, the second set of exercises aims to help you to enfold that part of the rape experience into the whole.

Write, draw and/or cut and paste to show what were the factors and circumstances that influenced your decision.

How did your family, friends, coworkers, counselors, or others support you, or not, in making your decision?

_____

_____

_____

_____

_____

_____

_____

Write, draw, and/or cut and paste to show how you felt about your decision at the time you made it.

Write, draw, and/or cut and paste to show how you feel about your decision now?

If you still do not feel comfortable about the decision that you made, please complete the following exercise.

After making a difficult decision, many of us continue to analyze it and rehash it. We go into the "I 'could have, should have, might have . . . " mental monologue. It is helpful to get those thoughts out of your mind and into the light.

In the space below, list what you "could have, should have, might have done" in the left column. Don't try to be rational. Any thought that is taking up space in your mind and mental energy, if even only slightly, is worth writing. In the column on the right, write how logical/illogical or rational/irrational that action would have been at the time. For example, in the left column you write, "I should have listened to my aunt Aunt Sarah." But after you think reasonably of that action you wrote in the right column, "Aunt Sarah is sweet, but not savvy." Empty that bothersome unproductive second guessing on the the page below.

Could have, should have, might have	Logical/rational reason for not doing so
_____	_____
_____	_____
_____	_____
_____	_____
_____	_____
_____	_____

How you feel about the way you were treated during and after the reporting process becomes a part of your healing. Police personnel, like all people, vary in sensitivity and caring. You may have been treated with great respect and made to feel safe, protected, and honored. On the other end of the spectrum, you may have been treated harshly and disrespectfully and made to feel as if you had done something wrong.

The following open-ended sentences will help you to clarify your thoughts and feelings about the way you were treated and how that treatment may still be affecting your life.

Complete these sentences to help you remember how you were treated and to express your feelings about that treatment.

I reported my rape at _____

_____

The surroundings were _____

_____

The police were _____

_____

The way they asked me questions was _____

_____

I'm glad that _____

_____

I'm sorry/angry/
sad . . . that _____

_____

This set of sentences will help you to express how you wish you had been treated.

I wish the police had been _____

_____

I wish the questioning had been _____

_____

I wish the surroundings had been _____

_____

I wish that _____

_____

_____

Add any other expressions of the way you wish other parts of the reporting process had been handled that might be part of your thoughts.

_____

_____

_____

Write, draw, and/or cut and paste to demonstrate your overall thoughts and feelings about the way the reporting process was for you.

Write, draw, and/or cut and paste to show how that experience continues to affect your life now.

Recalling the reporting process may have brought up some sensitive feelings. That is normal and natural. All feelings are appropriate, from gratitude to rage and everything in between. If what happened to you still has a negative impact on your life, please talk to someone who can help you sort it out and heal.

12
Prosecuting the Crime

Going through the judicial process is an experience in and of itself. Sometimes it empowers; sometimes it belittles. Whether you prosecuted or not and regardless of the outcome of that choice, trust that you made the best decision that you could at the time and under the circumstances. In retrospect, you may think that you should have/could have done it differently. Maybe that is so, maybe not. Making a decision of this magnitude is not easy. There often are emotional and rational factors, such as past experiences, the way you were brought up, your religious convictions, and your cultural background that although they are unrelated to the case, bear upon it, nonetheless.

You may have wanted to prosecute but couldn't because of reasons beyond your control. For example, the perpetrator was not arrested. There may have been a plea- bargain, or the district attorney's office concluded that there wasn't enough evidence. Many factors could have caused you not to prosecute. On the other hand you may not have wanted to prosecute but were compelled to do so, by your family or your friends or by the situation. No matter what happened, or why, it is normal for you to have thoughts and feelings about the incident. The purpose of this chapter is to help you to:

a) reconstruct the reasons you came to the decision that you did

b) feel good about it

c) review and integrate your experience

d) acknowledge the lessons you learned from the process

There are many factors that determine whether prosecution is a wise or possible course of action. First, we'll look at some reasons why survivors choose not to follow through with prosecution, and then we'll consider why some survivors choose to go ahead.

Once again, remember that there is no right or wrong. There are only your story, your circumstances, and your decisions.

Here are some motives for not prosecuting:

- to remain anonymous
- to safeguard someone else
- to protect the perpetrator
- fear of retaliation
- fear of being shunned in the community
- fear of being ridiculed and belittled
- fear of being accused of doing something wrong
- cultural or religious factors.

Add your own reasons.

_____

_____

_____

Here are some reasons survivors choose to prosecute:

- to be vindicated
- to obtain vengeance
- to feel empowered
- to protect someone else
- to "get him"
- to have the perpetrator suffer
- to have the truth be known

Add your own reasons.

_____

_____

_____

Describe in words or pictures what the experience of choosing to prosecute, or not, was like for you.

Support from family and friends significantly affects decision making of this magnitude. Let yourself remember what kind of support, or lack thereof, you received from these groups.

Describe the kind of support that you received while you decided to prosecute, or not to prosecute.

Your family

_____

_____

_____

_____

Your friends

_____

_____

_____

_____

Your coworkers

_____

_____

_____

_____

Your neighbors

_____

_____

_____

_____

The local rape-crisis center

_____

_____

_____

_____

The police

_____

_____

_____

_____

The district attorney

_____

_____

_____

_____

Use this space to add any not mentioned above.

_____

_____

_____

_____

Would you make the same decision now or do things differently?

_____

_____

_____

_____

How?

_____

_____

_____

_____

Why?

_____

_____

_____

_____

How would that decision/action have served you better?

_____

_____

_____

_____

Write, draw, and/or cut and paste what you think and feel now about your experiences associated with deciding to prosecute, or not to prosecute.

We hope that working on these exercises has convinced you that you made the right decision for you. Even if others might have decided otherwise, only you could have decided what was right for you then and what is right for you now. Your decision might be different today, but your circumstances today are quite different from what they were then.

Seeing a case through the judicial system can be overwhelming and the experience as varied as the individuals who participate in the process. Complete the sentences below.

What was your experience.

_____

_____

_____

_____

The assistant district attorney was

_____

_____

_____

_____

Other legal staff I had dealings with was

_____

_____

_____

_____

The judge was

_____

_____

_____

_____

The jury was

_____

_____

_____

_____

I'm glad that

_____

_____

_____

_____

I wish that

_____

_____

_____

_____

Use this page to write, draw, and/or cut and paste to illustrate your experience with the judicial system.

As with the other exercises in this book, reviewing the memory of your decision to prosecute or not to prosecute and the circumstances of your experience with the judicial process probably stirred some emotions. If you experienced relief, contentment, or a sense of pride, for instance, take time to acknowledge and honor those feelings and rejoice in them. If, however, you experienced some unpleasant thoughts and feelings, take the time right now to care for yourself. If you are unsure what you might do, refer to Chapter 1 of this workbook.

13
Changes and Adaptations

Life flows. We are constantly changing physically, mentally, and emotionally. As new experiences come into our lives, we adjust and adapt to contend with the new challenges that face us.

In this chapter, you are invited to examine the ways in which having been raped and the events that followed have required you to adjust and to adapt. How do you feel about these changes? Perhaps you experienced being raped and the events that followed with few, if any, changes. This sometimes happens. Martha was raped in her house by a man who followed her in through her kitchen door. She told her husband who was very supportive and loving. She talked to me a few times and came to the decision that it was an accident, that it was not about her, that she had better things to think about, and that she was not going to let this event change her life. She did stop using the kitchen door for a few months. End of the story. This course of action and feeling reflects who Martha is and how she handles her life and the tragedies that have befallen her over the years. She is not one to let things affect the way she has chosen to look at life and she tends to carry on as if nothing had happened. Like Martha, you may have decided to put the experience behind you and to continue with your life. This is neither a good way nor a bad way to handle a situation. It is one way, and we each have our own style of dealing with what life presents to us.

On the other hand, you may have made major lifestyle changes. Stephanie, who was raped in the parking lot as she left work in a big city, decided that she had enough of living with so much violence around her. She quit her job, moved to the country and works as an organic gardener. In retrospect, she views her rape as the motivation to live the kind of life that she always wanted, but she also continues to be nervous about big cities, and she will not wear skirts.

For some women, having been raped becomes a devastating experience that triggers a series of misfortunes. If this is your case, and you seem to be unable to put yourself back together, please, contact a professional to help you. Taking this step is an act of great courage, but you can do it.

Perhaps the changes you feel are more internal, such as a subtle change in how you regard yourself and how you relate to the world. You may even find yourself behaving, thinking, and feeling in ways that are unusual for you. Some changes feel positive, others feel disturbing.

As we move through the process of healing, we forge a new self. The metaphor that works for me is of a crystal glass that is shattered, then painstakingly put back together, piece by piece, with lead sutures holding the fragments. The original material is thus molded into a goblet of a much different design, strength, and beauty.

Some of the changes in you may have been minute, others great. Changes may be long-lasting or of short duration. Much depends on your basic personality; on the circumstances of your life at the time of the rape; on what actually happened; on the kind of support you received from family, friends, doctors, therapists, police, and others; and a multitude of other factors.

You may have noticed a change in your appearance or maybe there hasn't been one. You might have changed in how you feel about certain things, or how you react to events or other people. Perhaps you view the world differently now or have changed your environment, and how you do certain things and the importance you place on different situations. Perhaps you think none of these things have happened to you. The next exercises will help you to recognize the changes that have occurred in your life since you were raped.

Some of these changes may be directly linked to the rape, others not at all. After all, change is a natural, normal part of life. You may embrace and enjoy some of the changes, you may dislike some, and you may decide to alter other aspects still more. In any case, be kind to and compassionate with yourself as you complete the exercises.

Describe the changes in your personal appearance both right after the rape and now.

Right after the Rape

Hair   _____

_____

Clothes   _____

_____

Weight   _____

_____

Perfumes/   _____

scents/soaps   _____

_____

Others   _____

_____

Now

Hair   _____

_____

Clothes   _____

_____

Weight   _____

_____

Perfumes/   _____

scents/soaps   _____

_____

Others   _____

_____

How do you feel about these changes in personal appearance?

_____

_____

_____

_____

_____

_____

_____

_____

_____

Describe the changes in your lifestyle.

Right after the Rape

Home
environment   _____

_____

_____

Eating habits _____

_____

Sleeping habits _____

_____

Now

Home
environment   _____

_____

_____

Eating habits   _____

_____

Sleeping habits _____

_____

How do you feel about these changes?

_____

_____

_____

_____

_____

_____

_____

_____

_____

_____

If you are still having problems with any of these situations such as not being able to sleep, or oversleeping, under/over eating, living in an unpleasant or uncomfortable situation, please do seek help. These are normal difficulties after being raped, but, after a while, you should be able to resume a comfortable, satisfactory lifestyle.

Describe the changes in your activities.

Right after the Rape

Social activities   _____

_____

Leisure time   _____

_____

Taste in music   _____

                        _____

Taste in books   _____

                        _____

Taste in movies   _____

                        _____

Taste in sports   _____

                        _____

Others   _____

                        _____

Now

Social activities   _____

                        _____

Leisure time   _____

                        _____

Taste in music   _____

                        _____

Taste in books   _____

                        _____

Taste in movies   _____

                        _____

Taste in sports   _____

                        _____

Others   _____

                        _____

How do you feel about these changes?

_____

_____

_____

_____

_____

_____

_____

_____

_____

Describe the changes in your work situation.

Right after the Rape

Type of work   _____

                   _____

Location   _____

                   _____

Responsibilities   _____

                   _____

Schedule   _____

                   _____

Other   _____

                   _____

Now

Type of work   _____

                   _____

Location   _____

                   _____

Responsibilities   _____

_____

Schedule   _____

_____

Other   _____

_____

How do you feel about these changes?

_____

_____

_____

_____

_____

_____

_____

_____

_____

_____

_____

Describe the changes in the way you relate to people.

Right after the Rape

Relatives   _____

_____

Friends   _____

                        _____

Coworkers   _____

                        _____

Professionals   _____

                        _____

People in the   _____
community
                        _____

Now

Relatives   _____

                        _____

Friends   _____

                        _____

Coworkers   _____

                        _____

Professionals   _____

                        _____

People in the   _____
community
                        _____

How do you feel about these changes?

_____

_____

_____

_____

_____

_____

_____

Describe the changes in the way you view the world.

Right after the rape

_____

_____

_____

_____

_____

_____

Now

_____

_____

_____

_____

_____

_____

How do you feel about those changes?

_____

_____

_____

_____

_____

_____

Describe the changes about the way you feel about things.

Right after the rape

_____

_____

_____

_____

Now

_____

_____

_____

_____

How do you feel about these changes?

_____

_____

_____

_____

_____

_____

_____

_____

_____

_____

As you reflect upon the changes in your life since you were raped, some may still be painful or difficult to live with. You might feel glad about other changes.

Make a list of the changes in your life that you feel good about and tell how they have improved your life.

_____

_____

_____

_____

_____

_____

_____

_____

_____

Make a list of the changes in your life with which you are dissatisfied.

_____

_____

_____

_____

_____

_____

_____

_____

What could you do about the changes in your life that dissatisfy you?

_____

_____

_____

_____

_____

_____

Remember, sometimes changing the things we don't like in ourselves or our situation can take time. Planning how you can make a change is a huge step in the right direction. Sometimes, acceptance of the situation as it is at the time, may be the most beneficial change for the moment. Attitude towards a situation is a large part of its resolution.

With gentleness and compassion, take a few moments to review the changes that have occurred in your life since you were raped and to reflect on your present life. Acknowledge yourself for all the work that you have done and for the person that you are.

Returning to the metaphor of the glass and the goblet, I invite you to use the next couple of pages to express the kind of person you were and how you perceive yourself now.

Write, draw, and/or cut and paste to describe the glass that you were.

Write, draw, and/or cut and paste to describe the goblet that you have become.

14
Growth and Opportunity

The Chinese pictograph for "crisis" is a combination of the symbols for danger and opportunity. As a survivor of rape, you have gone through the danger, the physical, mental, and emotional danger, of the actual event. You faced the risks entailed in the aftermath, such as deciding whether to tell and whom to tell, whether to seek medical treatment, whether to report the rape, and whether to prosecute.

If a crisis is a dangerous opportunity, and you have weathered the danger, then you now have the opportunity to acknowledge and to honor the strengths and attributes that you already possessed and those that you have developed in order to cope with your rape and the events that followed. We all have different strengths. No strength is inherently better than another and none works all the time. Different skills are required to handle different situations. Gentleness can be as powerful as bravado. Shelving your feeling can be as brave a decision as facing them. Talking about your situation with someone you trust takes as much courage as keeping quiet.

The next exercises are designed to help you to recognize your skills and strengths and to give you the credit you truly deserve.

Write, draw, and/or cut and paste the skills you have that helped you to **cope** with your rape and its aftermath.

This is not the time to be shy or to underestimate yourself. If you are having trouble with this exercise, imagine that you are talking to a friend. What would you tell her?

Write, draw, and/or cut and paste to describe the skills and strengths that you developed as a result of having to deal with your rape.

Remember, any characteristic that enabled you to go through the process is a strength, whether it was stubbornness, yielding, letting others help you, etc.

Thinking back over the whole experience, what did you learn about yourself?

_____

_____

_____

_____

_____

_____

How will this information serve you in the future?

_____

_____

_____

_____

_____

_____

Add any other positive thoughts or feelings about your strengths.

_____

_____

_____

_____

_____

_____

When you have completed these exercises, take some time to acknowledge yourself. This may be difficult for you, too. The practice of honoring ourselves for our accomplishments is not inherent in our culture. We are taught not to brag about ourselves. However, you are not bragging, you are honoring your strengths and skills. Honor yourself in some way that has meaning for you. It can be as simple as taking a moment to acknowledge yourself, lighting a candle, making a cup of tea, as elaborate as planning an outing, or inviting a circle of women to share your accomplishments.

You may be feeling disappointed that you are not yet healed from the wounds to your mind, soul, and body. Give yourself time. We heal in layers. A deep wound to the body heals more quickly on the surface than the layers of tissue below. It is no different for any part of us, including our mind and our soul.

Part 2

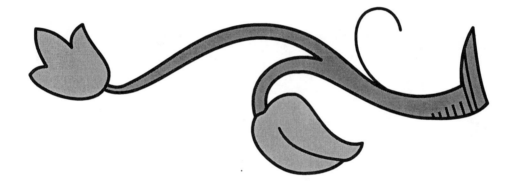

15
Medical Attention

You have come through the rape, and you are a survivor. One of the issues that faces you now is to decide which type of medical attention to seek. It is wise to get tests for sexually transmitted diseases including HIV and for pregnancy. Also if and/or when you prosecute, the information gathered by a medical person can be used as evidence and be important to your case.

You have several choices, such as the hospital emergency room or outpatient services, women's health clinics, or private gynecologists. If you were bruised, cut, or otherwise physically injured, the hospital emergency room may be your best first choice. You do not have to tell them that you were raped. You can go just for the treatment of injuries. However, if you tell them that you were raped, they will have the opportunity to gather evidence that is vital to prosecuting.

The following paragraphs describe each option. If you want help or more information, call your rape-crisis center. The personnel there should be able to give you information about the medical facilities in your area, make some calls for you and may even be able to have someone meet you at the hospital, clinic, or doctor's office if you'd like.

Hospital Emergency Rooms

Some have special rooms where rape victims can have more privacy. Tell the triage nurse when you come in. Some have specially trained personnel and procedures for examination, testing, and treatment of rape victims that are geared to lessen the anxiety of being in an emergency room and of having the medical exam.

You might want to call ahead of time, or have someone call for you, to find out what procedures the hospitals in your area follow. Rape-crisis centers, which often operate 24 hours a day, usually have this kind of information available and probably have established contact with hospitals that can facilitate your being there and getting the appropriate treatment.

Find out if your facility uses a "rape kit." A rape kit is a set of procedures and equipment used to collect and to protect the physical evidence of the crime. As a matter of policy, some hospitals routinely pass the evidence on to the police for use during a trial. Others store the samples for a certain amount of time. Emergency rooms are more likely to use this kit than are private clinics and physicians.

If you are on your way to a hospital emergency room immediately after your rape, and you want evidence gathered, the following procedures are recommended:

Personal Hygiene

The following are natural things to do. However, if you have not already done the following, **don't**

- wash your hands or face
- take a shower or bath
- wash your mouth or brush your teeth, specially if there was oral contact
- clean your finger nails
- urinate —— if you must, try to save the urine
- drink or eat anything
- comb your hair

Clothes

- Do not change your clothes.
- Bring a clean set of clothes. The hospital may want to keep your clothes for evidence.
- If you have already changed, bring your "old" clothes as evidence in a brown paper bag. Plastic, white, and colored paper bags could affect the substances that may be on your clothes.

In other words do not alter your appearance in any way. If you have already done any, or all, of the above, don't worry about it. These are just added helps to evidence collection. The main evidence is gathered by the nurse or doctor doing the examination.

Hospital Outpatient Services

Hospital outpatient departments are similar to the women's health clinics or a private doctor. The advantage is that many of them have walk-in services. The disadvantage is that you may have to wait a long time before being seen. Some will see patients by appointment only. Check with your local facilities for policies. They may or may not have a "rape kit" or special procedures for dealing with rape victims.

Women's Health Clinics

The best known women's clinic is Planned Parenthood, but there are many others that provide gynecological exams, treatment, and counseling. Many include counseling as part of their services. Some are pro-choice and will perform first trimester abortions. You can find such clinics in the *Yellow Pages* under "clinics," or check with your rape-crisis center. Most women's clinics will not call the police and most of them do not have "rape kits" available. Their services are confidential in the same way that the services of a doctor are confidential.

Most women's health clinics do not have walk-in appointments. You need to call ahead to make an appointment. Although you occasionally can get an immediate appointment, it may take a few days or weeks. When investigating what services a clinic provides you might also want to ask what policies and procedures they follow.

Private Doctor

If you already have a gynecologist whom you see for routine check ups, you might chose to go there. On one hand, you might feel comforted to have someone you know examine you. On the other, you might feel uncomfortable sharing that you were raped by someone you know.

If you don't have a gynecologist, or you want to see someone different, ask someone you trust for a referral, or call your rape-crisis center. The *Yellow Pages* are seldom a wise choice, because you have no idea of the caliber of professional you will be seeing.

Again, remember that it's okay to ask a relative, friend, or counselor to make the calls for you and to accompany you to appointments. You don't have to do this all on your own. You've just been through a major trauma and need assistance. You wouldn't expect someone who was in a car accident to handle everything by themselves. Taking care of yourself is what you need to do. Even if you don't look like you've been through anything, you have.

Use the space below to make notes to yourself of persons/clinics you might want to call, their phone numbers, any questions you might want to ask.

_____

_____

_____

_____

_____

_____

_____

Going to a doctor, hospital, or clinic can feel overwhelming and upsetting. Here are some suggestions from other survivors that many help make the experience easier for you.

- Have a friend or relative come with you.
- If you are going to the emergency room, call or have someone call ahead.
  - » Let the emergency-room personnel know you are coming. Many hospitals will provide you with some privacy and may assign someone who is specially trained to help you. It might make the signing-in process easier.
- Arrange for someone from your local rape-crisis center to meet you at the facility.
- Bring your walkman and your favorite tape, a book, needle point, knitting, a pad for writing, or drawing, or other activity to occupy your time in case you have to wait.
- Bring any object that feels comforting.
  - » A stuffed animal, picture, rock, piece of clothing, etc. (You can keep it hidden in a bag if you want.)
- Go to a facility in a neighboring town or neighborhood if you are concerned about encountering someone you know.

As mentioned earlier, it is highly recommended that you get medical attention. The exercises on the following pages are designed to help you decide whether to seek medical attention and which kind of medical attention is most appropriate for you.

If you are uncertain about whether to seek medical attention, the list below, compiled by other survivors, may feel comforting and help you to clarify your thinking.

Reasons for choosing to obtain medical attention

- I wanted to make sure I didn't catch a sexually transmitted disease.
- I wanted to find out about pregnancy.
- I wanted evidence gathered for possible prosecution.
- I had previously had good experiences with medical attention, it made me feel safer.
- I found it comforting to be checked out.

Reasons for choosing not to obtain medical attention

- I didn't want to be seen, to answer questions, or to be touched.
- I had a bad experience in the past.
- I felt that somehow I wasn't worthy of treatment.
- I thought that this way, by not taking this next step, I could make it all go away and I wouldn't have to deal with having been raped.

On the next page is a chart on which to write all your reasons for you to receive a medical check up, and all your reasons against having a medical consultation.

Reasons to Go   **Reasons Not to Go**

_____   _____

_____   _____

_____   _____

_____   _____

_____   _____

_____   _____

Which ones feel more compelling?

_____

_____

_____

_____

Which ones make more sense?

_____

_____

_____

_____

Why?

_____

_____

_____

_____

_____

_____

_____

_____

If you're still having doubts and feeling confused and uncertain, talk to someone you trust and whose opinion you respect, or call a rape-crisis center to talk to a counselor. Often this can be done over the phone.

Deciding to go is the first step. The second step is determining where to go. The next exercise is designed to help you make that choice.

Next to each type of facility, write the advantages and the disadvantages that are associated with going to that particular facility.

	Advantages	**Disadvantages**
Hospital	_____	_____
	_____	_____
	_____	_____
Women's Clinic	_____	_____
	_____	_____
	_____	_____
Private Doctor	_____	_____
	_____	_____
	_____	_____
Other	_____	_____
	_____	_____
	_____	_____

Now list the names, addresses, phone numbers, appointment times available, and any other comments for the facilities in the category that you have chosen. This should help you pinpoint which ones are your first and second choices. Again, remember that it's okay to ask for help in doing this.

If you want to do this exercise with more than one category, just repeat the process on another sheet of paper.

Category

Name	Phone #	Address	Times Open	Notes

_____

_____

_____

_____

_____

_____

_____

If you are experiencing a jumble of feelings at this time, don't worry. It's common and normal. You've just gone through major trauma. Whatever you are feeling and thinking is appropriate, even if it seems strange or weird to you. These thoughts feelings and behaviors are all a predictable part of Rape Trauma Syndrome (see Chapter 6).

In the meantime, take a break and relax, though that may sound easier said than done. Do something pleasant for yourself (even if this suggestion sounds ridiculous). Listen to some music, call a friend, read a book, watch a movie, anything that will help you take your mind off the immediate situation for a little while.

16
You Don't Have to
Be Superwoman

If I am not for myself, who will be?
If I am not for others, who am I?
And if not now, when?

Rabbi Hillel

The concept of being a superwoman has been ingrained into many of us. We believe that we should be able to handle any situation, and that reaching out means we're weak ---- and being weak is not acceptable. Well, you are not Superwoman. Nor can or should you be Superwoman. Superwoman exists only in fiction. She helps everyone and relies on no one. It's not human, possible, or healthy. As the song says, " Everybody needs somebody, sometime." No matter how capable and self-reliant you usually are, now is the time to reach out for physical and emotional support. To reach out and ask for help doesn't mean you are weak. It means that you are taking care of yourself and it is a gift to others to give them the opportunity to be loving and helpful.

Think about your family and friends. Whom can you depend upon? Not everyone can be helpful in the same way. One person may be great at doing practical things, like running errands, or making appointments, or finding things out. Another may be a great listener and provide emotional support but is too disorganized to get things done. Someone may live too far to provide help, but may be available if you need someone to talk to at 4:00 a.m., while your housemate, who may be willing to get up extra early to make your breakfast and drive you to work, will be a monster without eight hours of uninterrupted sleep.

The following exercises will help you to identify whom you can call upon for support and in what capacity. As you do these exercises, remember that you can always add names.

Write the names of relatives, friends, and other support people. Make sure to include people like a therapist, clergy, doctor, teacher, neighbor, coworker, and such. Next to each name write in how they can be of help.

Name   **How she or he can be of help to me**

_____

_____

_____

_____

_____

_____

_____

_____

Look at your list and think about your experience with each person on your list. How dependable were they? What do they do best?

_____

_____

_____

_____

Now, think about and list the things that need to be done. Write them **all** down, even the seemingly little things like making a phone call or getting groceries. Check the ones you can do easily. Next to each, write the name of the person(s) who could be of assistance. You may even have someone help you ask for assistance.

Things that need doing	Who can help
❑ _____	_____
❑ _____	_____
❑ _____	_____
❑ _____	_____
❑ _____	_____
❑ _____	_____
❑ _____	_____
❑ _____	_____

Asking for and accepting help and support may be difficult at first, but remember those are important steps towards your healing.

Now think of the things that you need. The things that will be emotionally helpful like having someone have dinner with you, take you to the movies, come and watch television with you, sleep over, or provide other support. Write down the things that would make you feel better. Next to each thing write the name of the person who could provide that comfort.

Things you need	Persons who could provide them
_____	_____
_____	_____
_____	_____
_____	_____
_____	_____

17
Reporting the Crime to the Police

Whether to report the crime to the police is the next decision that faces you. **Rape is a crime.** You are the victim of this crime. Your assailant, regardless of whether you know him, is a criminal. You may report the crime immediately after the rape or at a later time. Check the statute of limitation (that is the time you have in which to report a rape) with your local police department or your rape-crisis center. Whether you report the incident to the police is, of course, up to you. There is no right or wrong. It's a decision that can be influenced by many factors. Whatever your thoughts and feelings about your circumstances at the moment they are valid. However, as hard as this may be, you need to consider that your present decision may impact the events of the future. The thought of reporting what happened to you may feel totally overwhelming at the moment. You have just been the victim of a rape. You don't have to decide what to do right this second. Furthermore, you don't have to make the decision by yourself. Do give yourself the chance to talk with someone you trust or to call your rape-crisis center for support and guidance.

The purpose of this chapter is inform you of the ways you can report and to help you make the best decision for yourself.

Following are some of the ways in which reporting is done:

- Have the police meet you at the hospital.
  - » You can call the police and ask them to meet you.
  - » You can ask a relative, friend, nurse, social worker, or rape crisis counselor to make the call for you.
- You can go to the police station.
  - » You might want to call ahead, or have someone call for you, and let them know that you are coming.

» Ask a relative or friend to go with you.

» Ask for privacy if it will make you feel more comfortable.

» Going with or arranging to meet a rape counselor might also be helpful.

- You can request that an officer come to your house, a rape-crisis center, or any place that feels safe to you.

- Some police stations have officers who have been specially trained to work with victims of sexual assault. You can request one.

Use the rest of this page to make any notes about who to call, phone numbers, questions you want to ask, and other information that seems pertinent. And, again, remember that it's okay to ask someone else to do the leg work for you.

_____

_____

_____

_____

_____

_____

_____

_____

_____

_____

_____

_____

_____

_____

_____

_____

What Will Happen

Whatever you may be thinking about the experience of reporting the actual event, it seldom occurs the way it is pictured on television or in the movies.

The police will ask you many questions as to the who, what, where, when, and how it all happened. They will try to gather as much information as they can about you and your assailant. Some of the questions they usually ask are your name, address, telephone number; where you were; what you were doing before the rape, and what you did after; do you know your assailant and where he lives; what does he look like, have you seen him before, how did he approach you, what did he do to you? Some of the questions may feel quite intrusive, but asking questions is the way the police gain an understanding of what happened, of who the perpetrator was, and whether this report might help link him to other rapes. If a question feels inappropriate or too invasive you don't have to answer it.

This process may be an unnerving time for you. You may be asked the same questions over and over. Take your time and answer as well as you can. You don't have to feel pressured to provide information that you don't remember or about which you are unsure. You can always fill in the gaps later.

If you are being made to feel uncomfortable in any way, tell them. You should not be pressured in any way. You can take a break at any time. If you don't like the person who is asking the questions, you can ask for someone else. You can ask that a woman officer be in the room. You can ask to have someone you trust in the room with you. You can ask that the interrogation be done in a private room, not where other people are present or passing through. Respect your needs. You are there to help the police as much as they are there to protect and help you.

Reporting is your legal right, and it is important, even if others say that you shouldn't bother.

Many assailants threaten that they will rape you again if you report. The police may be able to give you protection. Furthermore, in most instances, there is no way for your assailant to know that you reported your rape, especially if he is a stranger. Additionally, statistics show that rapists seldom rape the same person twice. The exception to this is in cases of unreported date and acquaintance rape.

When you "report," you can ask that no further action be taken. Then, the information you give goes into the records. This information helps the police compile a "profile" of the assailant and will help fill in and complement information given by other victims as to what he looks like, how he usually operates, where he usually hangs out, etc. These clues can help the police find your assailant, arrest him, and possibly, prosecute him. To *prosecute* means to request that continued legal action be taken against the rapist after he is arrested. The next chapter talks about prosecution.

For the moment, however, let us return to the decision of whether to report your rape, as a crime, to the police. For most victims, it is much easier to report being raped by a stranger. Rape perpetrated by a family member or someone you know or care about, as in a date rape, is much harder to acknowledge or to report, but, it is equally important. If you feel bad about reporting someone you know, think about these facts: their behavior is criminal, they hurt you, they will most likely hurt others, and they need help to stop. Most likely, they also won't stop their criminal acts until someone forces them to do so. You may be that person. Many victims are unsure about reporting because they believe that, in some way, the rape was their fault.

It is important for you to remember that no matter what you were doing, where you were, what you wore, who you were with, and whether you were intoxicated, the blame still rests on the assailant. No matter what the circumstances, no one has the right to rape ---- to force sexual contact on anyone ---- at any time.

Forcible sexual contact is a crime whether or not there was actual intercourse. Those who commit the crime should be prevented from doing it again.

Let's explore the reasons to report, then the reasons not to report.

Reasons to Report

- To have your assailant arrested.
- To regain control of your life.
- To recover your financial loss for treatment. Many states have a Crime Victims Compensation Board which will pay for medical and psychological expenses that result from a rape. They also will cover some of the loss of possessions, earnings, and other damages due to the rape. Applications are filed with the Crime Victims Compensation Board of the state in which the crime occurred. A police report is necessary to qualify for benefits.
- To help other victims and to protect potential victims.

Add your own reasons. Don't try to be rational. Just list anything and everything that comes to your mind.

_____

_____

_____

_____

_____

_____

_____

_____

_____

Reasons Not to Report

- Fear that your living situation may be jeopardized if you do.
- Fear that it might make things worse in your life.
- Worry about facing ridicule or shame.
- Fear that you will not be safe.
- Desire to put the whole thing behind you.
- Distrust of the police.
- Fear of being embarrassed.

Add your own reasons. Don't try to be rational. Just list anything and everything that comes to your mind.

_____

_____

_____

_____

_____

_____

_____

_____

Which reasons feel more compelling?

_____

_____

_____

_____

_____

Which make more sense to you?

_____

_____

_____

_____

_____

Why?

_____

_____

_____

_____

_____

What decisions does that point you towards?

_____

_____

_____

_____

_____

Write what factors most influenced your decision.

_____

_____

_____

_____

_____

You know yourself, your present circumstances, your family, your friends, and your neighborhood. Reporting may be the best choice for you. Not reporting may be your best decision. What matters is, that you feel good about your decision.

Write, draw, and/or cut and paste to illustrate how you feel about the decision that you have made.

If you're still not sure about your decision, talk to someone who can help you clarify your issues. Get more information from either the police (you can call anonymously or have someone call for you), or from your rape-crisis center.

If You Have Decided to Report

If you have decided to report, we urge you to do so as soon as possible. The sooner the better. Crime-victims compensation boards have restrictions as to the length of time that has elapsed before you make a report. The statute of limitations, the length of time you have to report to the police, is longer. Check with your local jurisdiction, or with your local rape-crisis center, as there are differences from state to state.

Also, if you think you will want to prosecute, juries tend to look more favorably upon victims who report right away. However, if it has been a while since your rape, and you have decided that reporting is the right decision for you, don't assume that you are too late. Later is better than not at all.

If You Have Decided Not to Report

There is nothing that you need to do. You might still want to consider telling someone you trust so that you don't have to carry the emotional baggage of having been raped in silence. If you had been in a car accident, or if you had been robbed, you would most likely tell. Telling someone about your rape is just as important.

Like so many of the issues connected with the aftermath of being raped, deciding whether to report is not easy. Many factors must be considered and some of these may make sense only to you. You need to trust your own knowledge and validate whatever decision you make. Honor it. Reading this chapter and going through the previous exercises may have brought up or heightened some uncomfortable thoughts, feelings, and/or sensations. This is a healthy and a normal part of the aftermath of trauma. So, be kind and compassionate towards yourself. Practice TLC (tender loving care). Take some time to be with yourself, or with someone you trust, in a comforting way.

18
Prosecuting the Crime

The prosecution process begins after the crime has been reported, the assailant has been arrested and charges have been filed. It is the district attorney's office, not you, that decides whether to prosecute, based upon the amount and the kind of evidence available. Legally speaking, rape is a criminal offense that is perpetrated against the state. You, the victim, are a witness to that crime. There may be other witnesses, but you are considered the primary witness. If the district attorney's office decides to prosecute, it will represent you in court. You do not need your own attorney for criminal prosecution of a rape. Many district attorney's offices have lawyers who specialize in rape cases. Many district attorneys work in collaboration with rape-crisis centers to provide you with the best information and support possible.

The prosecution process can be lengthy and difficult. There are many steps, many conferences, and several hearings. You will have to tell your story many times. You may have to identify your perpetrator. The district attorney assigned to your case will prepare you to give testimony and will be there to support you during the process. A relative, a friend, and/or a rape-crisis center worker can also accompany you to court when you must testify. However, they may not be allowed in the room while you testify, except during the actual trial.

The prosecution process is seldom the way it is portrayed on television. Unless yours is a particularly notorious case, the proceedings take place in a small courtroom, with few, if any, spectators, and there most likely won't be any television cameras or reporters. Although the district attorney decides whether or not to prosecute, most district attorneys will be leery to move forward with a case if the victim is unwilling to cooperate. If the district attorney's office feels that yours is a good case, the attorneys will try to persuade you to prosecute. However, it is your choice whether to participate. Furthermore, you can stop cooperating at any point in the process. Of course, once started, it is a good idea to go through with the prosecution. But you don't have to if you don't want to.

Again, this is a time when you might want to talk to a rape-crisis center counselor. They are available to help and support you.

As a rape victim, you may also be able to bring civil charges against the offender, or, in some circumstances, against people who have allowed certain unsafe situations to occur, that may have facilitated the occurrence of the crime. To determine whether you have a valid civil suit, you need to contact a private attorney. If you do not know one, you can ask someone you trust for a recommendation, or you can contact your local rape-crisis center or the Bar Association of the town or state in which the crime occurred. Again, it is seldom a good idea to look for a lawyer through the *Yellow Pages*. It is not necessary to file criminal charges to file a civil suit; however it is helpful to your case, because it provides strong evidence of the occurrence of the crime.

The exercises on the following pages are designed to help you examine your ideas and feelings about the prosecution process and to help you make the appropriate decision.

In the space provided below write your reasons for prosecuting, or not.

Reasons to prosecute

_____

_____

_____

_____

_____

Reasons not to prosecute

_____

_____

_____

_____

_____

Which ones feel more compelling?

_____

_____

_____

Which ones make more sense?

_____

_____

_____

Why?

_____

_____

_____

Were you ever involved in prosecuting before this time? _____

If the answer is no, go on to page 164.

If the answer is yes, answering the following questions will help you put that experience into perspective and to notice how it might be influencing your present decision.

When and in what capacity were you involved in the prosecution process?

_____

_____

_____

_____

_____

_____

Write, draw, and/or cut and paste to illustrate what that experience was like for you.

How is that experience influencing your present decision?

_____

_____

_____

_____

What were the circumstances then?

_____

_____

_____

_____

What are the circumstances now?

_____

_____

_____

How do you think that the present experience would be similar?

_____

_____

_____

_____

How do you think the present experience would be different?

_____

_____

_____

_____

If you have not previously been involved in the prosecution process. Write, draw and/or cut and paste to illustrate your idea of what it would be like?

What aspects of this scenario feel positive to you?

_____

_____

_____

What aspects of this scenario feel negative to you?

_____

_____

_____

How do these factors influence your decision?

_____

_____

_____

What kind of support do you expect from your family, friends, community, coworkers?

_____

_____

_____

Do you think that your decision will affect your relationships? _____

How?

_____

_____

_____

Did the above exercises help you choose to prosecute? _____

List the factors that influenced your decision.

_____

_____

_____

Did the above exercises help you decide not to prosecute? _____

List the factors that influenced your decision.

_____

_____

_____

Neither decision is particularly better than the other, it is simply the decision that's right for you.

If you're still unsettled, take your time to consider all the present factors. Try to get as much information as possible from the district attorney's office and/or from a counselor at your local rape-crisis center. Sift through your images and fantasies of what it would be like to go to trial. These might help you determine whether your decision is based on facts, or on stories that you have heard from friends, seen on television, or read in books and newspapers.

As with the other decisions that you've had to make, this may have been relatively easy and unconflicted. On the other hand it may have been difficult, and time and energy consuming. We all have areas of ease and areas of difficulty. That's how it is. Do not compare yourself to anyone else or judge yourself. You did what you had to do, the way you had to do it, and made the decision that ultimately was right for you.

So, take some time to rest, to be gentle with yourself. If you're not sure what to do, check out the self-care chapter at the beginning of this book.

Other Books by Learning Publications

Johnson, Kathryn. *If You Are Raped: What Every Woman Needs to Know,* 2nd ed. Learning Publications, 1998.

Kercher, Glen. *Supervision and Treatment of Sex Offenders,* Rev. ed. Learning Publications, 1998.

Mayer, Adele. *Sex Offenders: Approaches to Understanding and Management.* Learning Publications, 1988.

McEvoy, Alan, and Jeff Brookings. *If She Is Raped: A Guidebook for Husbands, Fathers, and Male Friends,* 2nd ed. Learning Publications, 1991.

Parrot, Andrea, Nina Cummings, and Timothy Marchell. *Rape 101: Sexual Assault Prevention for College Athletes.* Learning Publications, 1994.

Rouse, Linda P. *You Are Not Alone: A Guide for Battered Women,* 2nd ed. Learning Publications, 1994.

Simon, Toby, and Bethany Golden. *Dating: Peer Education for Reducing Sexual Harassment and Violence among Secondary Students.* Learning Publications, 1996.

Simon, Toby B., and Cathy A. Harris. *Sex Without Consent, Vol. 1: A Peer Education Training Manual for Secondary Schools.* Learning Publications, 1993.

Simon, Toby B., and Cathy A. Harris. *Sex Without Consent, Vol. 2: A Peer Education Training Manual for Colleges and Universities.* Learning Publications, 1993.

Spence-Diehl, Emily. *Stalking: A Handbook for Victims.* Learning Publications, 1999.

Sullivan, John. *Licensed to Rape?* Learning Publications, 1999.